6/9₀

De

By Dick Davis

POETRY

In the Distance   1975
Seeing the World   1980
The Covenant   1984
Lares   1986

TRANSLATIONS

Attar: The Conference of the Birds   1984
   (with Afkham Darbandi)
Natalia Ginzburg: The Little Virtues   1985
Natalia Ginzburg: The City and the House   1986

CRITICISM

Wisdom and Wilderness: The Achievement
   of Yvor Winters   1983

EDITIONS

Thomas Traherne: Selected Writings   1980
Edward FitzGerald: The Rubaiyat of Omar Khayyam   1989

Dick Davis

Devices and Desires

New and Selected Poems
1967–1987

Anvil Press Poetry

Published in 1989
by Anvil Press Poetry Ltd
69 King George Street London SE10 8PX

Copyright © Dick Davis 1989

This book is published
with financial assistance from
The Arts Council of Great Britain

Set in Aldus
by Wyvern Typesetting Ltd, Bristol
Printed and bound in England
by The Camelot Press plc, Southampton

British Library Cataloguing in Publication Data

Davis, Dick, 1945–
   Devices and desires : new and selected
   poems, 1967–1987.
   I. Title
   821'.914

   ISBN 0–85646–201–1
   ISBN 0–85646–208–X Pbk

ACKNOWLEDGEMENTS

Some of the new poems first appeared in *Lares* (1986),
a limited edition published by Sea Cliff Press, New
York City and The Cummington Press, Omaha,
Nebraska. Thanks also to the editors of *Drastic
Measures, The Listener, New Poetry 1, Paris Review,
Poetry Book Society Anthology 1986/87, Poetry
Durham, Rialto, Spectrum* and *The Times Literary
Supplement*.

We have followed too much
the devices and desires
of our own hearts. . .

Contents

from THE COVENANT (1984)

NEW POEMS

from

In the Distance

(1975)

Bach's 'Capriccio sopra la lontananza
del suo fratello dilettissimo'

Distant, most dear; dearer, more distant than
Ever in life, this music that I hear
Can never reach to you, nor these words span
The waste to you, whom I still love and fear.

The Diver

to Michaelis Nicoletséas

The blue-cold spasm passes,
And he's broken in.
Assailed by silence he descends
Lost suddenly

To air and sunburned friends,
And wholly underwater now
He plies his strength against
The element that

Slows all probings to their feint.
Still down, till losing
Light he drifts to the wealthy wreck
And its shade-mariners

Who flit about a fractured deck
That holds old purposes
In darkness. He hesitates, then
Wreathes his body in.

The Shore

He feels against his skin
Throughout the night the pulse
Of her unchanging sleep:
Delicately, within
Her grasp and warmth, he rolls
Aside to watch the deep

Thought may not sound: her face
And body are a blur
Of breathing shadow, where,
Beyond that gentle pace,
He may by love infer
The darkness of her hair,

Her covered eyes, the shape
Of hands still touching his,
Her mouth: but nothing more.
If he, by stealth or rape,
Would seize her mind he is
Held helpless at the shore—

Impatient, lost: she goes
Untraced beyond the gleams
Of intellect, control—
He waits, but never knows
What demons or what dreams
Possess her voyaging soul.

Touring a Past

*'The ruins, which are not very remarkable, are
situated on an island which is almost impossible
to reach. . .'*

HACHETTE GUIDE TO THE MIDDLE EAST, p. 1003

Even from here I see
How stagnant and unused
The brackish waters lie,
As if the bank had oozed
This stream that sluggishly
Reflects the idle sky.

There is no boat to cross
From that ill-favoured shore
To where the clashing reeds
Complete the work of war
Together with the grass,
And nesting birds, and weeds.

I read that now there is
Almost no evidence—
No walls or pottery—
Of what I know were once
The walks and palaces
Love lent to you and me.

Scavenging After a Battle

Cold rimed on the metal,
The slam of the sea on the gravel—

Stone warriors and overturned horses,
He picks his way among corpses.

Diligently he
Severs gold, hacks the stones free

Of their rusting heraldic moulds—
Rubies; sapphires; emeralds.

Colour cupped in his hand; the sea
And the clouds cold grey.

Among Ruins

Rest here and fantasize the willing past
That like a lover answers to your mood:
You know her kind deceptions will not last
(And even now they only half delude).

But as nude bodies meet with stolen pride
And in their lust renounce all mental ills—
Leaving sad individual lives outside
The locked room where the animal fulfils

Himself, herself—so in this bright ruin
Sweet history shall tease and beckon you,
And as she moves seem free of ancient sin,
Half-lit, and only partially untrue.

Byzantine Coin

How many hands, vicissitudes,
Have worn this gold to the thin ghost
That gleams in the shopkeeper's palm?
A millennium flickers, eludes
Us, is gone, as we bend engrossed
In blurred words and a surface charm.

Diana and Actaeon

He strays from sun to shade
And hears his favourite hound
Cry in some distant glade
That the tired deer is bayed.

At once, almost, the sound
Cannot be placed: he peers
Distractedly around
At unfamiliar ground.

The vagueness that he hears,
The eucalyptus trails,
Chafe at his nascent fears—
This way and that he veers,

Trapped, simple flesh: details
Half-lost between the trees
Cohere, and reason fails.
The goddess stoops, unveils—

Then naked stands, at ease,
Tall in the swirling stream:
Her hair stirs on the breeze,
And as he stares he sees

Her eyes fix his. They gleam
With infinite disdain.
His dogs' jaws snarl, but seem
Elsewhere—till through the dream

He feels the gash of pain.

The Virgin Mary

All these oppressed her:
                    light's
Peremptory pure glare
In summer, and the weak
Pallor of winter air;
Men's breath against her cheek,
And fruitless unshared nights.

Her strange clothes hung in mute
Annoying folds. She dreamed
Of splendour, undefined.
Naked, her body seemed
The useless withered rind
Of some prodigious fruit. . .

As if a distant call
Abstracted her, she bore
Her days indifferently,
And waited vaguely for
One slight contingency
That would resolve them all.

Childhood

to Robert Wells

Imperceptible, at sunrise, the slight
Breeze stirs the dreaming boy, till silently
He edges free from sleep and takes the kite,
Huge on his shoulders like an angel's wings,
To climb the hill beyond the drowsing city.
Released, the first ungainly waverings

Are guided out, above the still valley,
Constrained to one smooth flow, diminishing
Until the pacing boy can hardly see
The dark dot shift against the constant blue:
He squats and stares: in his hand the taut string
Tugs, strains—as if there were still more to do.

Youth of Telemachus

It is a land he knows. White sunlight
Specifies each shrub and stone—
And as he moves his vacant sight
Restores him to the ways he's grown:

He is enclosed in reveries
No will can break, and where he goes
A child's unfinished fantasies
Dictate the paths that he will choose.

He rises in the dawn: the sun
Illuminates where he will pause
And where proceed: at his return
He sleeps and dreams his father's wars:

Until one evening he delays,
Past sunset, sunk in memory:
He sees the moon. rise and he stays:
All night he scans the changing sea.

Old Man Seated Before a Landscape

'generations, as the wind-blown leaves. . .'

In a strengthless wind the near leaves falter:
They are cold: frost will decide their posture.

To watch unsettles him: each separate
Discrete particular, an animate

Uncertain will claiming attention: no.
The distant unclimbed hills dissolve and glow

With evening light: the vague unfocused mass
In which particulars of rock and grass

Are lost and merged in indistinct coherence
Restores vague peace, and his awareness loosens

Toward sleep: his book slips: loose pages flutter
In the cold wind. He had been reading Homer.

Service

Mismanaged love, at large, made vagrant,
Uncontained; seeking the enormous land

Seen fleetingly, once manifest, now lost:
Seeking the defining rite, the service

That the heart could bend to—of rosary,
Or gun, or patient domesticity.

Love in Another Language

A stream irregularly dammed
    With unshaped stones
That swerve the current in its course—

    The meaning crammed
Through unfamiliar channels, in new tones,
    With a choked force.

Don Giovanni at the Opera

God is not here nor there, though there
    Breasts swell to the attack
Of Mozart, and her loose dark hair
    Spills on her naked back.

God is not here nor there, though there
    The new soprano sings
Betrayed Elvira's wild despair,
    Plucking his nerves like strings.

God is not here nor there, though there,
    In the interval, gin
Glitters, winks, and the dark girl's stare
    Is answered with a grin.

God is not here nor there, though there
    Sensation eases thought:
The whispers of a new affair
    Beguile, and he is caught.

Irony and Love

Irony does not save:
The knowledge that you repeat
The infantile indiscreet
Reactions of the dead

Does not save. Irony
Says nothing when her hand
Gestures the promised land.
Irony is the dead

Who are not saved but see
Magnificent bold Orpheus
Claim the incredulous
Soon-to-return Eurydice.

The Epic Scholar

What is his life? the library,
    Worn books minutely scanned,
The evening and the single meal.
    He dreams of the vast land.

He sees behind the Ur-text loom
    The dedicated band
Who, barbarous, inhabit him:
    He dreams of the vast land.

A scholar's indolence: the shelves
    Dissolve to endless sand;
Horizons touched, lost enmities:
    He dreams of the vast land.

His patience thins: minutiae:
    His predecessors planned
The complex text impeccably:
    He dreams of the vast land,

His solitary action there:
    O he can understand
His love's futility: but look,
    He dreams of the vast land.

North-West Passage

'To seek new worlds for gold, for praise, for glory'
SIR WALTER RALEIGH

The green sea lapped, a liquid jade.
That too was theirs, or soon. They saw
The drenched green dream of England fade

And fracture in the sluice and pour
Of Arctic waves. Their villages
Bobbed quietly, and were no more:

Small jagged ice-floes took their place
And nudged and clustered round the ship
As if they followed, keeping pace

With its unsteady yaw and slip.
Low cloud obscured the sky, and snow
Began to fall, and like a whip

Brine-soaked they felt the cold spray blow
Against their cracked unhardened skin.
They saw the raw wounds split and grow.

Ice glistened in the rigging, thin
And spectral as the silver veins
Threading the ore that they would win.

North-west: illimitable gains
Shone vaguely through the frozen mist
And they assuaged their bodies' pains

With hope, numb promises. North-west:
But slower now; beneath the weight
Of ice the ship would dip and list

As if the yards were animate
And leant in thwarted amity
Toward their final, restless, fate.

Men, silent, watched the ice-clogged sea
And felt their small ship shudder, strain,
And slow, and slow, perceptibly:

And in the night the livid stain
Of ice against the dark rose high
Above the watch, who saw disdain,

Malevolence, and in his cry
Of 'Icebergs! Icebergs!' heard that fear
He had suppressed, that he would die.

But ceaselessly, beneath the sheer
Harsh cliffs of ice, the helmsman's hand
Lay motionless, as if to steer

North-west through all his life. Low land
Appeared, an inhospitable
And lifeless waste, to port, ice-bound:

The sea became invisible
Beneath the sliding ice that scraped
The ship in rhythm to the swell,

Until the slowed hull trembled, stopped,
Stuck firm between the massive floes,
At last, irrevocably, gripped.

Their nights grew longer, and the snows
That swirled about the stranded hulk
Disguised the distant shore-line, froze

Their food, their friendship, boredom, talk;
Their limbs, their minds. Indifferently
They heard the timbers crack, the bulk-

Heads buckle, gape; for they could see
Slow scurvy undermine their friends
Insidiously and totally

As ice that saps and weakens, bends
And snaps their rotting ship. Their food
Exhausted, stubborn hunger sends

Them hunting, but no hopes delude
Their lonely search. As they return
Across the hard-packed ice they brood

On human flesh, and one by one
The lots are cast. They kill, they die—
And though the lots are cast again,

Again, uneaten bodies lie
Preserved till spring, then lapped and rolled
By waves beneath the Arctic sky;

And waves disperse their dreams of gold
Who had not thought the world could be
So small, so comfortless, so cold.

The Socratic Traveller

Beneath the inconsistent skies
He moves, in sun and sudden rain,
The rinsed air following, his eyes
Undaunted, as if unaware
Of what might turn aside their stare
And mitigate the real terrain.

He begs the truth of all he sees—
The city and the village, plain
And moorland stream, the crowded trees,
Each street, each desolate high hill—
He finds no meaning but he will
Not mitigate the real terrain:

He prosecutes his pilgrimage
Toward the sceptic's partial gain
Of seeing what is false—the gauge
Of truth becomes whatever he
Cannot discern as sophistry
That mitigates the real terrain.

Until he penetrates by slow
Degrees to ignorance, the vain
Obverse of all that he would know:
And, pausing, he is made aware
It is his constant presence there
That mitigates the real terrain.

Anchorite

He moves, in the debilitating heat,
Flesh wormed and riddled as an ikon's gold,
Light-headed from the lack of food, toward
The soul's oasis, an incorporal shade.

The Novice

An exiled Oedipus, he makes his way
Through the stunned crowd, sentenced by his own code:

Such sex and power were his, and what were they?
Sightless he stumbles toward the open road.

Narcissus' Grove

A place for the evasive, self-lockt stare,
The useless beauty that the world disowns:

Water sedulous over the grey stones—
The pines' sweet resin scents the sleeping air.

Living in the World

Abandoned dreams, of sainthood or rusticity,
The pure heroics that the child desired,
Disturb the sleeper, lapsed in promiscuity—
His will dispersed, and unappeased, and tired.

Littoral

Salt smoothes and sand obliterates
The trite, the once-dear vestiges

Mute hieroglyphs, the hulks of pomp
And sea-worn amulets of love.

Reading After Opium

Precise and indefinable: like scent
The drug diffuses, eddies, in his mind.

'God', 'love':
                    he gropes to what the words once meant,
As if these gentle pastures had been mined.

Names

Inapprehensible, the world: what was,
Once, almost palpable, is now become
The names of absences: tree, face, water.

I journey toward another absence, one
I dare not name, but whisper as I place
My steps, like a child's skipping-rhyme, 'Lord, Lord'.

from

Seeing the World

(1980)

Travelling

1 *Pastoral*

Wild lavender and mint;
                    the mind's bemused
Sheep browse—cropping the serious anecdote,
Eschewing the dust of small-talk.
                              Nearby,

Reason is a small boy who throws stones, sends
His yapping dog, to guide the errant flock.

2 *An Arrival*

Stranger, accept the little that is given—
The evening crowds, the quick unlooked-for smile
And the benediction of the sunset:
                              who knows
But the tryst with the unknown god is here?

Desert Stop at Noon

The house is one bare room
And only tea is served.
The old man, mild, reserved,
Shuffles into a gloom
Where mattresses are laid.
I sip, grateful for the cool shade.

His small son watches me,
Approaches, pertly smiles.
I know that thirty miles
Without a house or tree
Surround their crumbling shack.
I drink again, relax, smile back.

Water? and the boy's mother?
Both seem impossible—
Yet, here, my glass is full;
If I ask for another
The boy brings bitter tea
Then grins gap-toothed and begs from me.

And love? Impertinence
To ask. I could not grieve,
Born here, to have to leave:
But he, a man, years hence,
His life elsewhere, may weep
With need to see his father sleep

Again, as now he does,
In careless honesty—
Too old for courtesy—
Oblivious of us.
I pay, and leave the shade,
The dark recess these lives have made.

Night on the Long-Distance Coach

At last it is too dark to read.
I stare out on indifference,
A moonlit world that does not need
Our charity or deference.

And there my unfleshed face stares back,
Thin ghost through which far mountains show,
A palimpsest whose features lack
The constancy that lies below.

Below lie rock and scrub, the plain
Whence rodent eyes peer into mine—
An instant of inhuman pain
Deranges all I would define—

And I, and those I journey to,
Seem shadows without consequence,
A ghostly bustling to and fro
Through wastes of lunar permanence.

The City of Orange Trees

'The city filled with orange trees
Is lost', which, interpreted, meant
All conspicuous luxuries
Augur ruinous punishment.

This fitted what he knew. The zeal
For conquest, prayer, decays; the child
Mocks pieties he cannot feel
And children's children are beguiled

By comfort, gardens, literature.
Aesthetics dazes them, safe lives
Grow lax and soon they can endure
No one but slaves, musicians, wives. . .

Till to degeneracy the Lord
Sends one who, like their forbears, spurns
Mere taste as mannered cant. The sword
Falls and the plundered city burns.

*   *   *

Heir to three generations' learning,
He closed his book, his masterpiece.
Silk rustled as he rose, turning,
Ready to parley now for peace

With one beyond the city gate
Who, barbarous, impatient, vain,
No vows or presents could placate—
The world-conqueror, Tamburlaine.

Syncretic and Sectarian

If, unbeguiled by that suspicious wraith
Called Purity, we look with favour on
    The nebulous, syncretic faith
Of Shah Jahan's first-born, unworldly son—

(Translating Hindu scriptures into Persian,
Convinced the sadhu and the sufi were
    Lost brothers squabbling for the version
Of one tremendous truth) we must refer,

As well, to that blunt, younger brother who
—Contemptuous of vapid heresy—
    Was more than eager to pursue
(By fratricide) the wraith of Purity.

Memories of Cochin

an epithalamium

Through high defiles of warehouses that dwarf
With undetermined age the passer-by,
    We walk toward the ancient wharf,
Assailed by smells—sweet, pungent, bitter, dry:

The perfumed plunder of a continent.
To this shore Roman, Moslem, Christian, Jew
    Were gathered by the dense, sharp scent;
Absorbed now in the once-outlandish view

They camped by hills their children would call home.
So in the soil blurred Roman coins are found;
    Saint Thomas stepped into the foam
And strode ashore, and blessed the acrid ground;

Jews settled here when Sion was laid waste,
And Arabs edged tall dhows into the bay,
    Dutch burghers felt their northern haste,
Becalmed by slow siestas, ebb away. . .

So many faiths and peoples mingle here,
Breathing an air benign with spice and scent,
    That we, though strangers, should not fear
To invoke, in honour of our sacrament,

The sensual, wise genius of this place.
Approach, kind god: bestow your gifts on two,
    Your votaries, of different race
Made one, by love, by marriage, and by you.

Me, You

I am deceived
At first, but no—
You are asleep.
As if you grieved
For some lost glow
Of love, your deep

Dream moves your hand
To seek my skin
And there discover
The well-known land:
Somewhere within
Your brain a lover

Leaves you and you
Reach out to hold
Him close. I touch
Your body too—
As if he told
You what you clutch

Toward, your sleep
Grows still—and now
My hand explores
The silent deep
Of breast and brow.
My hand withdraws.

Now sleep is ours,
Quiet, till dawn
Will wake us to
The separate hours
And we are torn
Apart—me, you.

Marriage as a Problem of Universals

for Meera and Navin Govil

Marriage is where
The large abstractions we profess
Are put gently in their small place—
    The holist's stare
In love with Man has managed less
Than eyes that love one ageing face.

Marriage believes
The universals we desire
Are children of a worldly care—
    While Plato grieves
For stasis, the refining fire
Men pass through is the lives they share.

Marriages move
Between the symbol and life's facts,
From Beauty to this troubled face—
    Though what we love
Is Truth, Truth flares and fades in acts
Of local, unrecorded grace.

Don Giovanni

The unkissed mouth, unsubjugated eyes
Flower in the vacant air. . .
                              slashed down they rise

In mocking, gossipy, distracting swarms,
A ghastly hydra of unconquered forms. . .

He rides forward. Poor knight, poor travesty—
His quest uncertain, his adversary
At once monotonous and protean,
His loneliness immense, his armour gone
Except the shield,
                    which bears this sad device
'I know that something somewhere will suffice'.

'Vague, vagrant lives. . .'

Vague, vagrant lives, elusive, almost,
As the vision that they seek, at home
Nowhere. . .
             they pause before each landscape
With impartial eyes, as if they stood
Here only to collate, compare, then
Move again, assured. . .
                     drawn still nearer
To an understanding not yet found.

Government in Exile

Silence, and on the wall the photographs—
Farms, mountains, faces; the sad specifics
Corrode the heart, sharpen the will. Despair
Is shrugged away and stares one in the face.

Loyalty is poured out—a libation
To childhood villages, to stones, to trees.

Metaphor

Emotion flares, and is absorbed: almost
At peace you watch the opalescent west.
Light fades: a flock of birds starts up and wheels
And scatters in the sky, and recombines,
And settles as the first stars shine, intense
As loss, small points of agony, sharp signs
That glitter in the sky's immense grey waste.

Climbing

Enter the clarity you love—
The high thin air above the clouds
That in the wintry wind disperse
Like a mind clearing, like the fading
Of a loved illusion
                                    so that you see
The world with unencumbered eyes.

Here, at the summit, at your feet,
Stretches the black volcanic pool,
The dark Avernus of the self.

Dawn

You cannot say what sense it is through which
You understand but it is like the wind
That gently chill-ly tugs the desert plants
And leaves them undisturbed or like the air
That preternaturally reveals the hills
Or like the silence through which nothing sounds
Like words. Light spreads and speaks. You understand
It is that truth you need not understand.

Zuleikha Speaks

Gentle, then cruel—the same
Half-masked indifference
Dulls both. I say your name,
'Husband'. With what loathed sense

Am I yours, you mine? Night
Gives me to you but I
Shrink from its shameful rite,
Your energy and sigh,

The weight you think I love:
And in the day you watch,
Laugh, grumble, bargain—move
Beyond my woman's touch.

Now though you are not here.
I see the goats brought in,
The gilded dust, and hear
The world's unfocused din—

(Kids' startled hooves, boys' cries,
Somewhere a flute). The dim
Gold twilight weakens, dies.
I stay. I think of him,

The stranger—
                as reticent,
Ineffable, as is
This sun's unprized descent.
I know that I am his.

The cold wind stirs my dress.
The desert stars appear.
My husband calls. I bless
His name, but shall not hear.

Simeon

Luke II.26

How long now since
The vow was made. . .
Yet still he haunts
The temple's shade

Silent to those
Who say he dreamed
The angelic face.
Its splendour gleamed

More harshly than
The sacral knife
Caught by the sun,
And seared his life

To a blank daze
Of memory. . .
The half-glimpsed face
Of certainty.

As if that pause
When Abraham
Through lawless tears
Beheld the ram

Had been delayed
For centuries,
The falling blade
As on a frieze.

St Christopher

Curled fingers tighten in his curly hair:
But if, by any prescience, he knows
The nature of that burden He must bear
Whom now he bears, no recognition shows.

The weathered body and tenacious mind
Venture like partners with but one intent—
Lo, they are one, as cautiously they find
The safe stones through the unsafe element.

And thus, subsumed by what he does, made sure
That though his task is humble it is good,
He navigates toward the further shore—
Secure in skill and patient hardihood.

Winter

Your moment comes, inapprehensible.
Autumnal cold pervades the mountain pool;
The tense, still surface glistens; it is ice.
I peer, but cannot see what lives or dies.

Quotidian despair, I feel your cold lips
Searching me in the dark, your soft hand grips
With an enormous strength: I tremble, yours.
It is your hand that guides me now, explores

The vacant world for me.
                            I walk at night,
Possessed by the cold: on a building-site
Smoke from the watchman's fire smarts in my eyes:
Brief greetings clash, like gravel thrown on ice.

Withernsea

Stones, sand, I have not seen in fourteen years;
A place for childhood's self-communing tears,

For wandering. I walked the moonlit beach
An adolescent whom no waves could teach

The simplest truth of life, that nothing lasts:
I scavenged among poetries and pasts

For something glittering, precise and sure.
In winter-storms gigantic breakers tore

The cliff's vermilion mud into the sea.
The weakening edge seeps vaguely, constantly.

A Recording of Giuseppe de Luca (1903)

The record's hiss—so dense
You hardly hope to hear
The voice rise sweet and clear
Beyond its violence—

Seems like the sea-wash of
Time's old opacity
As it indifferently
Obscures the things we love.

But with what poignant strength
The voice soars free of time—
The young man in his prime
Still careless of the length

Of laggard years ahead,
Of that attrition which
No beauty can bewitch. . .
The youth so long now dead.

False Light

See where the landscape glows and flares
Lit by the beacons of desire—

As faces grouped about a fire
Give back the light that is not theirs.

Opening the Pyramid

Though you recall the emphatic starlight
When the angels said, 'Follow, we shall lead',

Irony, like the free air and sunlight,
Crumbles the mummy of each simple creed.

Wittgenstein in Galway

O come unto these yellow sands
Alone.
   The slow work of his hands,

Secluded by sad policy,
His hut opposed the breaking sea

Whose meaningless unchanged refrain
Might one day still the circling brain.

   * * *

Things that could never be thought of
Were metaphysics, anguish, love.

And though his tamed gulls swooped for bread
He lived, like us, inside his head

Locked out of that vast privacy
Of stones and sand, wild gulls and sea.

An Entry

'When one is frightened of the truth (as I am now) then it is never the whole truth that one has an inkling of.'

WITTGENSTEIN: NOTEBOOKS, 15.10.1914

To what strange sum could you be reconciled
That could atone for consciousness adrift
In grandeur it can never comprehend,

For suffering, for death?
                              What glimpse beguiled
You of our fear? What hand disclosed what gift
In token that blind passion has an end?

Two Epigrams on Victory

1

    Wotan and Prospero
Grown wise in tribulation know
    Whose is the victory,
And envy his simplicity.

2

Life narrows to the things you did not mean;
The endless vista is a painted screen.

Now, like the Count in *Figaro*, you see
Forgiveness where you ogled victory.

Love

Later her heart will blur with pain

(He sleeps. Her hand strays in his hair,
Impulsive, indolent.
                    She says,
'I love you' to the morning air.)

Now the years say nothing to her.

To Exorcize Regret

Grant the patience to accept
What the heart would still reject

May the distance be mere space
Grant the grace to need no grace

May flesh be flesh—
                    never again
Source and symbol of such pain.

Desire

Of the violence of that pain
What poor traces still remain—

This I learnt: the wry technique
Of avoiding what I seek.

Phaedra and Hippolytus

She felt the virgin's tentative
Thin lips brush stiff against her own—

Reluctant flesh, that would disown
Mere human need, and could not live.

Rembrandt's *Return of the Prodigal Son*

Age instinct with wisdom, love, bends towards
The sensual man, the penitent, and clasps
Him lightly by the shoulder-blades. In rags
The latter kneels and rests his close-cropped head
Against the Father's chest. Some watch, and one,
Whose face is lit, old as the Father, looks
With unobserved compassion at the scene.

His comprehension is the artist's own:
His silence and the Father's flood the frame
But cannot quite subdue the young man's sobs,
The fixed, sad past; the waste that love would heal.

Rembrandt Dying

What have I known?
The darkness I perceived
Beyond each face invades my mind,
I have been shown
The night of the bereaved
In which all men are blind.

But I recall
Old faces marred, their eyes
Outstaring that obscurity—
Awaiting all
Life yet may ask with wise,
Unbroken, dignity;

And the young Jew
Who was my Christ, in whose
As-if-omniscient, worn face
Compassion grew—
Where patience could peruse
The sufferings of a race;

And Hendrickje
Who taught me tenderness,
So that the proof of all technique
Was to convey
Love's truths—light on a dress,
Or on her turning cheek.

All these are past—
The darkness wells in me;
Though grief and ignorance increase
And must outlast
My will, yet memory
Is thankful for lost peace.

Leonardo

whose Last Supper *began to break up*
in his own life-time

My years were given
To permanence—
The arrested dance,
Emblem of heaven.

Decay invades
The icon of
Eternal love:
My emblem fades

Like human skin:
The wrinkles grow
As if paint too
Partook of sin.

Late, late I see
The meaning of
Incarnate love,
Eternity.

On a Painting by Guardi

Slowly the chill lagoon
Returns to flood these noisome ponds;
Grotesque, dense weeds festoon
The ruined arch with airy fronds

In whose shade scavengers
—Tenacious as the trailing weeds—
Time's ghostly avatars,
Indifferent to the grace that feeds

Their chance cupidity,
Draw strength from glory in decay.
Great Mutability,
All here declares your mordant sway.

I gaze, hardly aware
Of this overt, didactic aim:
Rather the misty air,
The blank, amorphous shore proclaim

An eye in love with blurred
And insubstantial forms, a mind
By evanescence stirred—
A suppliant of the undefined,

The pale marsh-haze of noon;
And one who in each breeze could see
—Ruffling the chill lagoon—
The tremor of mortality.

Epitaph

I betrayed and I was betrayed.
Wistful for righteousness I added to
    The world's evil. Invoke my shade
With gentleness; this grief will be yours too.

Maximilian Kolbe

O crux ave spes unica

Secure, afraid, I contemplate
The fearless necessary fate
Of one who, undisturbed by crime,
Became himself his Paradigm.

from

The Covenant

(1984)

Fräulein X

And it turned out that with her thanks for the
poison Fräulein X had still one more request:
would the friend sing Brahms's 'Vier ernste
Gesänge' before they parted.
DIARY OF RECK-MALLECZEWEN, DECEMBER 1938

Unseen, preserved beneath dark velvet, lie
Pale water-colours fugitive to light—
Displayed to none but friendship's gentler eye,
The sanctuaries of her sequestered sight—

Views of the Rhine and of the Holy Land,
Deep vistas of the spirit's need and rest:
Frail on glass shelves Venetian glasses stand,
The keepsakes of a life secure and blessed.

Now, in this last desire, she redeclares
Old faith in what is hers—Judaic psalms,
The German tongue: that heritage she shares
—Immutably—with Luther and with Brahms:

And though that sheltered world her childhood knew
Is shrunk to a dark room, though in the street
The mob bays hatred to the German Jew,
This covenant survives, beyond defeat.

In the Gallery

O patria mia!

One drawing held her; it was of
An indistinct but Eastern view
And had no special charm: her hand
Strayed to the glass as if she knew
The contours of that barren land
And could not stare at them enough:

I saw her beauty then, the love
Made steady in her exiled eyes:
Those lines were faint as memory,
Effaced as the elusive sighs
That scarcely broke her reverie;
I watched, withheld, and could not move.

Portrait Painter

If, in the middle-aged
Worn face now given to
His stranger's scrutiny
He sees—unbidden, true—
Regret stare unassuaged
From posed formality—

Her need and loss, a life
Of compromise made plain,
His thoughts are not the rush
Of sympathy for pain
But tone and palette-knife,
The texture of this brush:

And, glancing up, his gaze
Meets nothing of the heart
But colour, shade, and gloss—
The problems of his art;
While from the canvas blaze
Discovered need and loss.

What the Mind Wants

Young aspens mirrored in a stream;
A guileless evanescence, an
Unguided turning to the wind.

But also the persistent weight
Of glassy water, the steady
Pressure that seems barely moving;

The windless, slow, reflective depth.

The Jigsaw

for Sarah Davis

The portrait of the princess lies
In scattered fragments on the floor;
Crouched over them a young girl tries
Edges that would not fit before,

That sulk recalcitrant. . . ah there
Two pieces kiss: a greyish mass
That could be clouds or that patch where
Her dress half hides the shadowed grass.

The afternoon wears on: she sifts
And sorts; a piece is placed, withdrawn;
She sits up suddenly and lifts
Impatient arms. A stifled yawn.

And stoops again. Here no one wins,
It is a world you make and enter.
The edge is finished—now begins
The serious business of the centre.

A face emerges and young hands
Lie loose against grey silk; the eyes
Are guileless: almost there, she stands
Bent slightly forward in surprise.

Annunciation

Thin-shouldered, shy,
And much alone—
Anxious to screen
The monotone

Of her young life
From avid eyes,
The curious gaze
Disarmed by sighs,

By silence. . . but,
At heart, ashamed—
As if she knew
That she were blamed

For some dark sin
Unspecified—
As if the flesh
That broke her pride

Were penance for
An obscure fault
Not to be cleansed
In her tears' salt.

*

The morning lightens
Through poplar trees—
Her flushed skin takes
Dawn's sober breeze

As promise of
The known and real
To which she would
But cannot kneel.

And the light deepens
Beyond the line
Of glittering trees;
Their thin leaves shine

Till they are lost
In whelming light
Like water breaking. . .
She shields her sight

And hears the words
That justify
Her flesh, her life. . .
The unearthly cry

That battens on
Her faltering heart,
Naming her pure,
Elect, apart.

Four Visitations

Baucis and Philemon

Life lies to hand in hoe, spade, pruning-knife,
Plain wooden furniture and wattle walls,
In those unspoken words 'my husband', 'wife',
In one another's flesh which still recalls

Beneath the map of age their savoured youth.
It is an ambience in which they move
Having no need to grasp or grub for truth;
It is the still persistence of their love.

That one should die before the other's death
And drain the world of meaning is their fear:
Their hope, to draw together their last breath
And leave the sunlight on a common bier.

Life is the meaning and the bread they share;
Because they need no Gods, the Gods are there.

Semele

I imagine an English Semele—
A gawky girl who strayed beyond the town
Picking at stalks, alarmed by puberty. . .
Who by the handsome stranger's side lay down

And when he'd gone lay still in meadow-sweet
Knowing herself betrayed into the world—
Soft flesh suffused with summer's placid heat,
The clement light in which the ferns uncurled.

Both faded; meeting him again she sought
For that half-apprehended, longed-for power—
The glitter haunting her distracted thought
That seemed to peer from every leaf and flower,

The glory of the God. . . the girl became
The landscape's ghost, the sunlight's edgy flame.

Jacob I

This mother's darling, picksome in his pride,
Who lives by smiles, deceit, dumb-insolence,
Is sent out to secure a fitting bride
And takes the road in high self-confidence.

By noon there is no road—no shadows move
But his; the desert light glares hard and clear,
A lucid proof that he is owed no love,
That what pervades his solitude is fear.

The young man sleeps, his head propped on a stone,
Exposed to starlight and the vacant skies:
The angels climb, descend, and he is shown
Their ladder's length drawn up from where he lies.

First light, and cold air chills the dreamer's face
Waking to silence, in an empty place.

Jacob II

By sunset they had reached a shallow stream:
The women crossed and he was left alone
Unable to advance. As in a dream
A man with features known but scarcely known

Stood in his path and in the dusk they closed,
Strained sinew against sinew silently:
Who was the stranger whom his strength opposed,
The dark shape jealous of his liberty?

Dawn came, and locked within their stubborn fight
The traveller knew whose arms withheld him there;
'Bless me' he cried, 'Bless me before the light
Dissolves your substance to resistless air'

And one whom strength and skill could not confound
Was forced by benediction to the ground.

St Eustace

At dusk in the dark wood
The stag I'd harried stood—
Its wet flanks flecked with blood

The antlered head held high
As if not he but I
Were hunted here to die;

Between his tines the air
Grew solid to my stare:
The cross of Christ hung there—

I marked where he had bled;
Bright on his thorn-crowned head
The blood shone newly shed—

And as the moonlight broke
Through ash and smothering oak
The dead man moved and spoke.

Getting There

Now you approach the long prepared for place
The language you have learnt, the map you know
Seem childishly inadequate to show
Its obvious, unformulable grace.

But you were told that it would be like this
—An interim, an emptiness—a state
In which, like an expectant child, you wait
Not knowing what it is you must not miss.

Uxor Vivamus. . .

The first night that I slept with you
And slept, I dreamt (these lines are true):
Now newly-married we had moved
Into an unkempt house we loved—
The rooms were large, the floors of stone,
The garden gently overgrown
With sunflowers, phlox, and mignonette—
All as we would have wished and yet
There was a shabby something there
Tainting the mild and windless air.
Where did it lurk? Alarmed we saw
The walls about us held the flaw—
They were of plaster, like grey chalk,
Porous and dead: it seemed our talk,
Our glances, even love, would die
With such indifference standing by.
Then, scarcely thinking what I did,
I chipped the plaster and it slid
In easy pieces to the floor;
It crumbled cleanly, more and more
Fell unresistingly away—
And there, beneath that deadening grey,
A fresco stood revealed: sky-blue
Predominated, for the view
Was an ebullient country scene,
The crowning of some pageant queen
Whose dress shone blue, and over all
The summer sky filled half the wall.
And so it was in every room,
The plaster's undistinguished gloom
Gave way to dances, festivals,
Processions, muted pastorals—
And everywhere that spacious blue:
I woke, and lying next to you
Knew all that I had dreamt was true.

Travelling

You live for landscapes scudding past, the sense
That what sustains you is mere transience;

And for the dew immobile in each dawn—
The one clean stillness everywhere reborn.

A Short History of Chess

When chess began in India
The bishops charged as elephants,
The queen was still a minister
And both were clearly combatants

In battles secular and male.
Who claims that Eastern ways perplex?
It took the West to twist the tale
To strategies of faith and sex.

On Epigrams

This neat, egregious house-style
Parades its insights pat, on time:
It smiles a very knowing smile. . .
Here comes another fucking rhyme.

(Its *double entendres* are subtle, supple—
'To fuck' here means, of course, 'to couple'.)

The Householder's Bonfire

Splashed paraffin: the avid first flame licks
From crumpled paper to the heaped dead sticks.

I step back to avoid the swirling sparks;
My neighbour comes and badgers me with Marx—

Das Kapital, the crumbling bourgeois state;
My garden's tidy now—I close the gate.

A Letter to Omar

1

I stood beside the ghastly tomb they built for you
And shuddered with vicarious, mute guilt for you;
Are concrete columns what they thought you meant?
I wanted wine, a glass turned down, drops spilt for you.

A sick child reads (his life is not imperilled—
He sucks the candied death-wish of FitzGerald);
I was that child, and your translated words
Were poetry—the muse's gaudy herald.

Was it for you I answered that advertisement
Before I knew what coasting through one's thirties meant?
If so I owe my wife and child to that
Old itch to get at what your Englished verses meant.

Thus in your land I doled out Shakespeare, Milton—
Decided I preferred sheep's cheese to stilton
But knew as much of Persia or Iran
As jet-lagged fat cats sluicing at the Hilton.

My language-teacher was a patient Persian Jew
(I pray that he survives), a techno-person who
Thought faith and verse *vieux jeux*; he thought me weird—
He learnt my loyalties and his aversion grew.

Love proved the most effective learning lure and not
His coaxing tact: my girl required the score and plot
—Explained in halting, pidgin syllables—
Of our first opera (which was—aptly—*Turandot*).

When I had said, in crabbed words bare of ornament,
What *La Bohème*, *The Magic Flute* and *Norma* meant
She married me; my Persian was still bad
But now I knew I knew what 'nessun dorma' meant.

We set up home. . . but I feel more than sure you
Would nod assent to Dr Johnson's poor view
Of tulip streaks (*Damn all particulars.* . .)
And I desist—I wouldn't want to bore you.

2

You left the busy trivia unspoken:
Haunted by vacancy, you saw unbroken
Miles of moonlight—time and the desert edge
The high-walled gardens, man's minute, brief token.

And if I revelled in your melancholy
(Like mooching through the rain without a brolly)
It was the passion of your doubt I loved,
Your castigation of the bigot's folly.

Besides, what could be more perversely pleasant
To an ascetic, hungry adolescent
Than your insistent *carpe diem* cry
Of let conjecture go, embrace the present?

And all set out (I thought so then, I think so now)
In stanzas of such finely-wrought, distinct know-how
They were my touchstone of the art (it is
A taste our pretty *literati* think low-brow).

Such fierce uncertainty and such precision!
That fateful metre mated with a vision
Of such persuasive doubt. . . grandeur was your
Decisive statement of our indecision.

Dear poet-scholar, would-be alcoholic
(Well, is the wine—or is it not—symbolic?)
You would and would not recognize the place—
Succession now is quasi-apostolic,

The palace is a kind of Moslem Deanery,
But government, despite this shift of scenery,
Stays as embattled as it ever was—
As individual, and as sanguinary.

The warring creeds still rage—each knows it's wholly right
And welcomes ways to wage the martyrs' holy fight;
You might not know the names of some new sects
But, as of old, the nation is bled slowly white.

3

Listen: 'Death to the Yanks, out with their dollars!'
What revolution cares for poet-scholars?
What price evasive, private doubt beside
The public certainties of Ayatollahs?

And every faction would find you a traitor:
The country of the Rubaiyat's creator
Was fired like stubble as we packed our bags
And sought the province of its mild translator.

East Anglia!—where passionate agnostics
Can burn their strictly non-dogmatic joss-sticks,
And take time off from moody poetry
For letters, crosswords, long walks and acrostics;

Where mist and damp make most men non-committed,
Where both sides of most battles seem half-witted,
Where London is a world away and where
Even the gossips felt FitzGerald fitted;

He named his boat *The Scandal* (no misnomer. . .)
And fished the coast from Lowestoft round to Cromer,
One eye on his belovèd Posh, and one
On you or Virgil, Calderon or Homer;

Then wrote his canny, kind, retiring letters
To literature's aggressive, loud go-getters—
Carlyle and others I forbear to name
Who had the nerve to think themselves his betters;

You were the problems (metrical, semantic)
From which he made an anglicized Romantic—
The perfect correspondent for his·pen
(Inward, mid-century, and not too frantic);

As you are mine in this; it makes me really sick
To hear men say they find you crass or merely slick;
Both you and your translator stay my heroes—
Agnostic blessings on you both!
                              Sincerely, Dick.

November 1982

Exiles

The two friends fill their time with chess: black plays
Decisively—white dithers and delays,

Picks up a pawn, stares, scowls, then puts it back;
He sees that his spectacular attack

Has turned into a tedious defence.
He cannot win but keeps up the pretence

Of caring how he loses and to whom.
The wives are chatting in another room;

Their rumours rise in disconnected scraps—
'and gold'—'but X was shot'—'the prince perhaps'—

'and she got out with nothing, so she says.'
White sees a move that prettily delays

Black's victory. . . 'my dear, that's just her joke.'
'No, no—she claims she's *absolutely* broke.'

Black pauses now and white turns round to shout
'Sweet, who are you two gossiping about?'

Two East Anglian Poems

Trattando l'ombre come cosa salda
DANTE, PURGATORIO XXI. 136

With John Constable

Slow-rotting planks and moody skies;
I look with your impassive eyes

Whose tact is love for what is there—
The worked soil and the moving air,

The reticence of grief: I hear
Through silence your dead voice draw near—

Those words you gave to Ruisdael's art,
'It haunts my mind, clings to my heart.'

Edward FitzGerald

East Anglia, a century ago:
    I see FitzGerald bow
    To Attar's *Conference*
        As I do now

Leaning through silence to a dead man's mind,
    A stranger's pilgrimage
    (As is the book we read)
        To a blank page—

An immanence, remote, but quickened by
    An old, ill scholar's breath:
    I see you wrest this life
        From brother death.

The Tribe of Ben

How easy now to mock
Those who wrote looking back
To rare Ben Jonson's line—
Firm royalists to a man

Unfitted for the claims
Of chiliastic times,
Preferring penury
To the trimmer's smooth way.

Filed epigram and lyric
Held Fanshawe, Lovelace, Herrick
From lazy shame; each sought
In his obscured retreat

Not rage or grief but grace,
An undeluded peace.
Hear how such passion gives
Perfected verse its voice.

A Photograph: Tehran, 1920s

How false, incongruous, each prop
That crowds into your photograph—
The stiff, fake flowers, the painted drop
To signal opulence (park-gates
Your shoulder half obliterates),
The draped and tasselled table-top

Against which you benignly lean.
A slight smile ghosts your bearded face
As you confront the strange machine
Which traps you in your mullah's robe
(A signal now that half the globe
Can snigger at and call obscene).

Your gaze holds mine: I know that you
Were never rich, depraved, or mad;
That at your death a rumour grew
Of unemphatic sanctity;
That your frail legend troubles me;
That all the signals are untrue.

Richard Davis

. . . minding to have sent to Qazvin Alexander Kitchin,
whom God took to his mercy the 23rd October last: and
before him departed Richard Davis one of your mariners. . .

HAKLUYT, PRINCIPAL VOYAGES OF THE ENGLISH NATION

Our mariner's last landfall was this shore:
My namesake stood, four hundred years ago,
The empty Caspian at his back, and saw
A shelving view I intimately know—

Clean, silent air and noble poplar trees,
A marshy plain beyond which mountains rise,
The snow-line and the sky—all this he sees—
The colours fresh and calm before his eyes.

Fresh as your fading figure in my mind:
You look back to your little ship, then stare
As if the riches you had hoped to find
Were somehow present in the limpid air.

You walk towards the limits of my sight—
I see you stumble in the dusty light.

On an Etching by J. S. Cotman

I wept to see the visionary man
DRYDEN'S VIRGIL

There is no richness in this scene,
No life to answer his abstracted stare—
And what we take it that these emblems mean
Is but the index of his inward care;

The summer-house will always stay
About to fall, the river make no sound
As Lethe-like it bears his strength away
And lapses to the darkness underground;

And poised above the silent flood
The couchant lion waits, a mask of stone,
Impassive by the tree that will not bud,
The spell-bound youth, beleaguered and alone.

The landscape is an open grave
At which the artist and his subject gaze;
When acid eats the plate, his skills engrave
Wanhope, a mind that falters and decays.

Childhood of a Spy

Much earlier than most he found
Most things are not as they appear;
The mousy child who makes no sound
Lives in a haze of smothered fear—

Where is he safe? Reality
Is something glimpsed through misted glass;
A closed, adult conspiracy,
A frontier post he may not pass.

Truth is a secret and he learns
Its lonely code; the bit lip trembles
But says nothing—compassion turns
To hatred that a smile dissembles.

The frontier will be down, his fear
A state ubiquitous as air;
And, vindicated, he will hear
Their cry of candour and despair.

Near Coltishall

for Michael Riviere

Dark on the evening sky
(Though one gleams coldly bright
Caught by the sun's last light)
The thunderous aircraft fly
Into their deepening night:

Distracted from my page
I watch each passing plane—
The virtue of Montaigne
Is innocent to gauge
The wrath that they contain.

O privacy, retreat!
What fastness is secure
From that pervasive roar,
Who shall escape defeat
From what we dream of war?

(The village where I read
Is but a reference
On some chart marked 'Defence'—
Roofs overflown at speed
And of no consequence.)

Which would you choose, my lord—
The cant of government,
The smug cant of dissent?
Or would you turn toward
Your book's long argument

That wisdom is to know
How blindly we descend
To where no arms' defend
Our ignorance from no
Imaginable end?

Mariam Darbandi

1956–1983

How frightened you were once
—And not so long ago—
When late one night we took
Our pathway homeward through
The churchyard where you saw
Grey gravestones row on row;

And afterwards we teased
Your childish, tense alarm
And mocked the way you clung
Against your sister's arm
As if you sensed the dead
Reach through the moonlit calm.

Dear child, I see you now,
Dear helpless fugitive—
To guide you past that place
What could I now not give?
The taint was in your blood
That would not let you live.

Earth holds you in her arms
And soothes you of your fear
And it is we who turn
To see the dead appear;
Who listen for the voice
We know we shall not hear.

Reading

The last page read you pat
With thoughtful tenderness
    Your novel's spine—
How much I'm moved by that
Improbable caress
    Which I thought mine.

I copied it from you?
You picked it up from me?
    Who knows which way
The gentle gesture flew. . .
It marks that privacy
    We both obey.

My Daughter Sleeping

Your eyelids are so thin
That as you sleep I see
The eyeballs dart within
That near transparency
Of blue-veined, restless skin.

What do you dream, my dear?
Already after less
Than five quick months your fear
Is fear at which I guess:
I kneel as if to hear

The whispered testament
Of what I cannot know—
My listening head is bent
To silence trapped below
That thin integument.

A Christmas Poem

*Written for the 1982 Carol Service
of Nene College, Northampton*

One of the oxen said
'I know him, he is me—a beast
Of burden, used, abused,
Excluded from the feast—
A toiler, one by whom
No task will be refused:
I wish him strength, I give him room.'

One of the shepherds said
'I know him, he is me—a man
Who wakes when others sleep,
Whose watchful eyes will scan
The drifted snow at night
Alert for the lost sheep:
I give this lamb, I wish him sight.'

One of the wise men said
'I know him, he is me—a king
On wisdom's pilgrimage,
One Plato claimed would bring
The world back to its old
Unclouded golden age:
I wish him truth, I give him gold.'

Mary his mother said
'I know his heart's need, it is mine—
The chosen child who lives
Lost in his Lord's design,
The self and symbol of
The selfless life he gives:
I give him life, I wish him love.'

Abandoned Churchyards

The long grass covers
Untended graves—
Deep in its airy caves
Drowse summer lovers:

Flesh is subdued
To simple needs.
Think, where the rank grass seeds,
Love was pursued.

Hearing a Balkan Dance in England

The music gives itself, retreats:
Your mind's involuntary eye
Dazzles with fluttered handkerchiefs
Against a clear, Levantine sky;
In a quick pause the bride receives
Her groom's first kiss. The phrase repeats,

Repeats; again they dance.
                          And you,
A stranger at the wedding-feast,
Caught up in happiness, were there
Until the circling rhythm ceased—
As now it ceases and the air
Of Norfolk's sky glows Iznik blue.

Translating Hafez

NORTH WEST FRONTIER, 1880S

for V. L. Clarke

I see the man I conjure—at a doorway
Bathed for a moment in the evening light
    And watching as the sun
    Descends behind bare hills

Whose shadow blurs, and renders substanceless,
Parade ground, barrack, flag-pole—the low step
    On which he stands; 'the hour
    Of cow-dust', but no herds

Are brought in here to shelter from the dark:
The bright, baroque commotion of the sky
    Is simplified to dusk
    In which the first stars shine

Like an admonishment that stills the heart.
He enters the dark house: though he is here
    By accident he makes
    His being of that chance,

Set down within a country which he loves
And which, he knows, cannot love him—so that
    His homage is a need
    Become its own reward

Unprized as that which Aristotle says
Souls nurture for the irresponsive God:
    A barefoot servant brings
    The oil-lamp and his books

(And in another dispensation he
Would be that grave, respectful, silent child).
    Moths circle him and tap
    The lamp's bright chimney-glass;

Now seated at his desk he opens text
And commentary; he dips his pen and writes
    'It is the night of power,
    The book of grief is closed. . .'

Exile

I turn from longing to the tasks life gives.
Beneath all surfaces your river flows—
I call you Grief. I shun you and I hear
Your murmur as I give myself to sleep.

New Poems

Acedia

A lumbering, bumpy bullock-cart
Deep in the selfish provinces:
Your mood lurches and sways, over
Ruts, into potholes; you are flung
From side to uncomfortable side.
Goading the beast does no good, nor
Does yelling. It's started to rain.
This would be risible if there
Were someone to share the joke with.

6 A.M. Thoughts

As soon as you wake they come blundering in
    Like puppies or importunate children;
What was a landscape emerging from mist
    Becomes at once a disordered garden.

And the mess they trail with them! Embarrassments,
    Anger, lust, fear—in fact the whole pig-pen;
And who'll clean it up? No hope for sleep now—
    Just heave yourself out, make the tea, and give in.

'And who is good?. . .'

And who is good? The man who does least damage?
The saint who labours to transcend the human mess?
Often enough it's some poor conscience-stricken wretch
    Terrified of his own unhappiness.

I Have Been Here. . .

I recognize this place;
Another face stares through your face.

This is and is not you;
Her thin lips parted as yours do.

You speak with her veiled voice;
I tell myself there is a choice—

Nothing insists that I
Enter the storm's deceptive eye.

*   *   *

You put a record on—
Bruckner's contumacious passion

Breaks over me: I think
Tread water, ride it out, don't sink.

Undine

Evasion led him to a moonlit glade
But she was waiting there and drew him down
To the stream's brink beneath the thickened shade;
White water parted, and her white hair spread
About her body like a billowed gown.
Thin fingers tugged at his; as he obeyed,
Gingerly feeling for the rocky bed
Which was not there, he knew that he would drown
And let his whole weight sink. She kissed him then,
Her gentle mouth on his sucked out his breath
Which he was glad was gone. He did not hear
The liquid trickle of her laughter when
She broke alone into the air, or fear
The sudden depth where he encountered death.

Jealousy

To hear her talk about her friends
Is like glimpsing across dark gardens
Their lighted room, from which you are
Excluded; such kindness reigns there
In the bright warmth; you see a burst
Of laughter that you cannot hear.

Or it is being shown a blurred
Photograph of some unreachable
Good place: *look, there are olive trees*
And the beach where we swam—we slept
In that white house. . . You finger it,
The glamour of a life not yours.

Wisdom

The common wisdom is 'Accept what's given':
What's given is a long unhappiness,
A purgatory that cannot lead to heaven.
And O yes we accept it, more or less.

With Johnson's *Lives of the Poets*

to R. L. Barth

He wrote these quick biographies
To be instructive and to please;
   In them we find

Among judicious anecdotes
The apt quotation that denotes
   A taste defined

And wrested from this record of
His irritable, captious love
   For failed mankind—

From fear, from his compassion for
Insanity, the abject poor,
   The world's maligned.

He laboured to be just, and where
Justice eluded him his care
   Was to be kind.

Read generously—as once he read
The words of the indifferent dead.
   Enter his mind.

Janet Lewis, Reading Her Poems

The tape begins. A few pages are shuffled
Then her voice is there—old now, clear, unruffled,
Unassertive, going again among
Words given order when the heart was young:
The cadences are like that vanished race
They would evoke, leaving almost no trace
On the after air; gentle, evasive,
Too modest to accuse or to forgive,
Declaring simply this was here, and this,
Which is gone now—the bright frail edifice
Of summer stripped in time's storm.

                                                  But I share—
As the tape plays—her sense of sunlit air,
Of glades where uncoerced humanity
Knew wisdom as a kind of courtesy.

Ja'afar

The exiles' newspaper; plots, squabbles; I
See nothing here for an outsider's eye

Until '. . . and the late Ja'afar Modaress.'
How did you come by death? But I can guess.

I heard your thin, harsh voice excoriate
The lies of literature and of the state,

Then you laughed, shrugged; and what could laughter do?
You were not thirty when they murdered you.

I take your one book down; its flimsy cover
Reads *Short Stories: The Children's Games are Over.*

Middle East 1950s

This is a revolutionary photograph—
The crowded faces stare beyond the frame.

All but one: he looks into the camera,
An anonymous, middle-aged man holding
His daughter who turns her back to us, pressing
Her curls against his shoulder. Behind them
Soldiers gesticulate, crowded on a tank.

How open his face is: you read there hope,
Fear, decency. You see what is betrayed.

Ibn Battuta

Near the beginning of his first journey
The great traveller (who was to suffer
Shipwreck, the loss of all his wealth, his slaves
—On whom he doted—and his son; who was
To fight with pirates, brigands, be received
By princes as an equal and be laughed at
As a pauper; who was to see the known world
And its wonders) near the beginning
Of his first journey he tells us how
In company with a caravan of travellers
He approached a city, and how a crowd
Of well-wishers and relatives came out
To welcome them, so that each man was greeted
By a face he knew, except for him,
Ibn Battuta, whom no one greeted
Because he was a stranger there, and how
This knowledge was borne in on him, and how
He wept.
    When the book is closed this picture
Of the young man in his twenties weeping
—And not the princes, slaves and shipwrecks—
Is what stays with you
       so that you almost feel
Across the centuries the pressure of
Your hand against his arm, and hear
Your own voice raised in greeting.

Chebutykin

(in Chekhov's *Three Sisters*)

If I drop the clock it shatters—
Can I swear that this is true?
Never mind though, nothing matters.

Somewhere, someone vainly chatters
—How to live and what to do—
If I drop the clock it shatters.

No one listens: madam natters
—Dresses, servants, babies, flu—
Never mind though, nothing matters.

A household crazy as hatters. . .
No? . . . I haven't got a clue.
If I drop the clock it shatters.

I suppose my life's in tatters. . .
To be honest that's not new.
Never mind though, nothing matters.

Kindness comforts us and flatters—
Nothing else will see us through.
If I drop the clock it shatters.
Never mind though, nothing matters.

To the Muse

I can't complain
If you disdain
    To visit me—

Too often I
Tried to deny
    Your quiddity;

'She is a way
With words,' I'd say—
    'A competence

In what we make.'
A fool's mistake.
    My punishment's

To see you now—
Dark eyes, smooth brow,
    Your slim form turned

From me; cold, real,
Inviolable.
    Well, I have learned.

Magic

The child steps carefully
    Over the cracks
And at the corner sees
No bears—he can relax.

Grown older now, he says
    It's childish rot
But pulls white petals off—
She loves. . . She loves me not.

The next step is to cheat:
    'If I can climb
That hillside in an hour,
If I can find the rhyme

I need, she loves me'—and
    He does; but she
Doesn't. This is the Fall
Into Contingency;

He puts such magic by,
    Walks carelessly
Toward the messy future:
His poems do not rhyme.

Making a Meal of It

No point in murmuring
Against the life you live,
No point in hungering
For what Fate cannot give;

No point in calling up
Vast, empty words like Fate—
The table's set, sit down
And eat what's on your plate.

The Sentimental Misanthrope

You get things clear, define a space,
And find you hate the human race:

But act *gemütlich*, let things slide,
And it's yourself you can't abide.

Made in Heaven

They bring to one another what they are
Which is obscurely what was done to them:
The poise of the angelic predator,
The blank hunger that cannot say *Amen*.

Heresy

This is your heresy—
To translate and displace.
Your long desire to see
Salvation in a face

Unstable as your own
Is to be blind to what
Is literal blood and bone;
To worship what is not.

The Departure of the Myths

Now that the series of
Tottering bedizened
Edifices goes toppling
And tinkling into
The distance, surrounded
By singers and saltimbanques,
By outriders who curvet
Their horses and flourish
Bright, fabulous weapons—
We cannot deny that
The silence is (as
They grinningly warned us
It would be) unnerving.

But almost immediately
It's broken; a child
Is wailing somewhere—
And look, there it is
Grubby and rubbing its eyes,
About five years old,
Of indeterminate
Sex, left behind by
The glamorous, vanishing,
Self-absorbed caravan that
Now, as we watch, grows small
In the sunset.
                Suddenly
We see how ridiculously
Heedlessly cruel
That gross splendour had become—
How could it have touched us?
We hate it and rush
To console the distraught
Child who stubbornly
Evades our caresses and
Bawls for its mother.

Evening

At the lawn's edge the wood
Promises solitude.

Wet, tangled undergrowth
Has crept across the path

Where fox and badger go
Oblivious of you.

This is unhappiness
Where you must not trespass.

Turn back to the bright house,
Your child asleep upstairs,

Her face illumined by
The night-light's quiet glow.

Household Gods

Not books and pictures, no; although their sense
Must be the context of benevolence.

And not, no not, 'the sweepings of bazaars',
The clutter of our different, dying cultures.

Moments, not objects; the impalpable
Embodiment of what we hope is real.

The children's clothes untidy on a chair;
Voices absorbed in what they know and share.

The house silent at night, unspoken love.
Your book slips down; you sleep and do not move.

Lares; the bits and bobs of privacies,
Scraps, trivia; the heart's allegiances.

Afkham

I wanted otherness
And met your gaze, in which the world shone unreproved;
You were the world itself,
The uninterpretable strangeness to be loved.

Notes

THE CITY OF ORANGE TREES (page 42)

In *An Introduction to History—The Muqaddimah,* Ibn Khaldun quotes and explains the proverb with which this poem opens. The meeting that ends the poem occurred outside the walls of Damascus in 1401.

SYNCRETIC AND SECTARIAN (page 43)

Dara Shukoh, the eldest son of Shah Jahan, translated the *Upanishads* into Persian with the avowed intention of finding common ground between Islam and Hindu beliefs. In 1659 he was murdered by his younger brother, who later became the emperor Aurungzeb, the most fanatically zealous of all the Moghul emperors.

ZULEIKHA SPEAKS (page 51)

Zuleikha is Potiphar's wife. In one interpretation of the story Zuleikha represents the human soul wedded to the world (Potiphar) but 'illicitly' in love with the beauty of God, represented by Joseph.

WITTGENSTEIN IN GALWAY (page 58)

'(In 1947). . . he left Cambridge and settled for a while in Ireland. . . in a seaside hut in Galway, where the fishermen remarked on his ability to tame birds.' Anthony Kenny, *Wittgenstein.*

MAXIMILIAN KOLBE (page 67)

In Auschwitz this Polish priest voluntarily took on himself the death sentence passed on another prisoner.

Index of Titles